THE ADVENTURES OF
HENRY LEE BEAR

by Mimi Muldoon

illustrated by Lori Orlando

Trilogy Christian Publishers A Wholly Owned Subsidiary of Trinity Broadcasting Network
2442 Michelle Drive Tustin, CA 92780

Manufactured in the United States of America
10 9 8 7 6 5 4 3 2 1
Library of Congress Cataloging-in-Publication Data is available.
ISBN: 978-1-64088-373-4
E-ISBN: 97-1-64088-374-1

This book belongs to:

_____

Mama had three little bears and oh how they would dance, each and every time the violin came into her hands.

Henry Lee, bear number three, thought if he could play a tune, the other bears would dance divine so, off he ran into his room.

He dusted off his saxophone and played each note so carefully and when he sprang out from his room, he shouted out with glee! "Oh, Mama Bear, Papa Bear, come see what I can do, I practiced very much last night, all alone in my room."

Mama gathered all her cubs to come into the kitchen, great suspense filled the air as Henry Lee held his first audition!

"Twinkle, twinkle little star" was the song that he had studied but, when he blew into the Sax it sounded very muddy.

No one danced and no one clapped, no one thought he had a chance! The bear cub family tried real hard to think of what to say?

Papa Bear stepped forward with words to cheer his cub that day: *"Oh, Henry Lee, don't be dismayed, the saxophone is not for you, but if you go back to your room, here is what I think you should do...Ask the Lord if by some chance he can find another way, to help you find an instrument that he thinks that you can play!"*

With his spirits low and his saxophone in hand, Henry Lee understood that he must find a better plan. He brushed his teeth and combed his fur and rehearsed the words his Father had stirred.

"Lord, I am just an average cub, number three to be exact, do you think there is another gift that you could find for me per chance?"

Days went by, and not an answer, Henry Lee felt that his life would become a disaster.

Then one day, after school, a Musical Angel appeared *"Oh, young cub, do not fear, I know what God can do! Sit down at the piano bench and let the Lord use you! Yes, the Lord he heard your prayer that day when you asked him for a special gift and I have come to raise you up with all that you have wished!"*

Henry Lee looked real shocked to see
an Angel before his eyes...He stuttered
& stammered... then fell over with
laughter... for the Joy of the Lord had
changed his disaster!

So off he ran into his home to gather all into the kitchen, Henry Lee told each of them how God gave his life a new direction! *"Jesus filled my heart with Joy, with Words & Melodies. I Can Play the Piano now and I can even sing! I shall sing for you my song and life will never be the same, the Joy of the Lord is inside my heart and I have been truly changed!"*

His family watched and listened close to hear the cub sing from his throat, it wasn't like the saxophone or Mama's violin, Heaven blessed the bear cubs voice and how his loved ones cheered!

Yes, from that time and from that moment, how his life did change, Henry Lee now talks to God every single day.

The Joy of the Lord became his strength and you can have it too! Just talk to God from your heart and he will surely bless you.

The End

CPSIA information can be obtained at www.ICGtesting.com
Printed in the USA
BVIW120028210819
556339BV00033B/335

9 781640 883734